Discovering New Jersey Wineries

A Travel Guide to New Jersey's Wine Country

By Kevin M. Atticks

resonant publishing

resonant publishing
Baltimore, Maryland

Printed in the United States of America by
Data Reproductions Corporation, Auburn Hills, Michigan.
This book is printed on acid-free paper.

Library of Congress Card Number: 00-190955
ISBN: 0-9668716-6-9

First Edition
10 9 8 7 6 5 4 3 2 1

Photos by Kevin M. Atticks
Sketches by Nickitas Thomarios
Maps by Brian Schumacher
Edited by Judith M. Dobler
Assistant Editors: Terry Atticks,
Mary DeManss, Alicia Dunphy
Design by resonant design

*Those parties involved in this publication take no responsibility
for errors, typos or misprints. Every effort was made to
ensure the accuracy of information included in this book.*

resonant publishing

resonant publishing
Baltimore, Maryland

This book
is dedicated to
my mother, Terry,
a woman of
immense spiritual strength
who has guided me tirelessly
personally and professionally;

and to
my father, Ralph,
a man of
diverse interests and passions
who has given me endless support
on this and all other projects.

Thank you both for imparting
the best of your best...

Beer is made by men,
wine by God!

— *Martin Luther*

Table of Contents

New Jersey Wineries

Wine Trails
& Regional Suggestions

Good Information

Acknowledgements

The following people have provided me with invaluable information during the preparation of this book:

Gary Pavlis, Frank Salek,
Richard Higgins, Midge Boyd

The following people deserve special recognition, for their friendship and guidance have meant much more than they know:

Andy Ciofalo
Mary DeManss
Judith M. Dobler
Carol, Aedan and Alicia Dunphy
Andrea Hirsch
Kathy & Bob Hirsch
Meg Keegan
John McGraw
George P. Miller
John Mohan
Brian Schumacher
Nickitas Thomarios

*Thanks to the families and staff of every winery –
your patience and cooperation brought
this project to completion!*

Wine is sunlight,
held together by water.

— *Galileo*

Introduction

I wasn't surprised the first time I heard about New Jersey wines. Taking questions at a booksigning in promotion of my first book, *Discovering Maryland Wineries*, I hit a nerve. "Maryland wine is some of the best wine grown on the East Coast," I said in response to a pointed question about the quality of the state's wine.

"Well, then, you haven't been to New Jersey lately," spouted a man, defensively, as if I had just insulted his mother. Rather than start a shouting match, I asked him to tell me about his state's wine after the event.

And oh boy, did he. For a good 30 minutes.

He raved about all of the wines, especially those from a new winery whose name he couldn't think of off the top of his head.

I had no idea what to think about his views, but he was persistent enough to persuade me to visit my first New Jersey winery the following weekend. Just out of curiosity, of course. I entered the state hoping for the best but expecting little.

All it took was a two-hour departure off the turnpike before I was convinced of the merit of New Jersey wine. First to Amalthea Cellars in Atco, then to Tomasello Winery in Hammonton, and on to Renault Winery in Egg Harbor City.

Visits to these wineries were not what convinced me to write this book. It was the numerous conversations – rather, debates – with New Jersey residents trying to convince *them* that their fine state made even finer wine. The word has to get out somehow!

I continued my tour and not once was I disappointed with my discoveries.

In every discipline there are legends. New Jersey is a veritable breeding ground for legends in winegrowing. For years I had heard stories about a few of the renegades, rebels and recluses that made New Jersey's – and the East Coast's – wine industry so remarkable. Well, they're truly amazing: their ideas, winemaking skills and sheer confidence in every move they make were, at times, daunting.

As you visit the wineries, you'll meet these visionaries – many of whom have overcome more hurdles as winegrowers than they'll ever let us know.

If you're not from New Jersey but have driven through it to/from other regional metro areas, you've most likely been on the New Jersey Turnpike. And for many people, that's the prevailing impression of the state: lots of road, oil refineries, and one big airport.

All it takes is a 20-minute departure off the highways to see what New Jersey is truly about. A day in New Jersey's countryside can make a believer out of anyone. On a spring day the region emanates natural beauty with lush green farms, feathered flocks of native birds, and more farmers' markets than you'll ever need.

The spectacular diversity of the landscape adds to the state's invigorating spirit. From the sandy soils and shorelines of south Jersey to the vast forests and climbs of the northwestern part of the state, you'll never tire of traveling.

The wineries – and the people who own and operate them – are as distinct as the terrain. If you're on the hunt for fine wine, you'll find it at every winery. If you're searching for a fun event to pass your time, many of the wineries book events each weekend during

There's a feeling of timelessness on and around the Jersey shore.

the summer and fall months. If you're simply looking for a unique place to relax and enjoy a glass of professional-grade homegrown wine, look no further than the Garden State.

This a book not just about wineries, but about the whole concept of New Jersey's wineries. Visit the Musconetcong Art Gallery at Alba Vineyard, enjoy a fine six-course meal at Renault Winery, or attend the annual hunt for the elusive morel mushrooms at Four Sisters Winery, and you'll only begin to get a feel for the breadth of New Jersey wineries.

The places described in this book are much more than just wineries, they're places where you can temporarily disconnect from the status quo and do something different.

In each chapter you'll find a recipe or two; some from the wineries, some from other sources – but all very good. I can say I've gained a few healthy pounds from this book already! It's always been my theory that wine simply complements food, and vice versa. Try these recipes and I'm sure you'll agree.

Just a beautiful snapshot of one of New Jersey's scenic vineyards.

Also, take note of the art found throughout the book. All are sketches by Nick Thomarios of Akron, Ohio. He's an old friend of mine who graciously volunteered his art for my first book. So many people commented on his insightful drawings that I pleaded with Nick to create some more for *Discovering Lake Erie Wineries*. He did, and we received even more praise. And now, with *Discovering New Jersey Wineries*, Nick is premiering even more new work.

I hope you take this book with you on your travels throughout the state. Take advantage of the restaurant and B&B suggestions in the back to plan the perfect getaway. Or keep it in your glove compartment for those impromptu "just driving through" visits to wineries. Either way, may it introduce you to experiences you'll remember for vintages to come!

Kevin Atticks

Kevin Atticks
November 2000

Enjoy!

New Jersey Quality Wine Alliance

One of the most exciting things to happen in New Jersey's wine industry in recent times is the institution of the New Jersey Quality Wine Alliance (NJQWA). This designation was initiated by the Garden State Winegrowers Association, in cooperation with the New Jersey Department of Agriculture and the Rutgers Cooperative Extension.

The NJQWA was created to give consumers something to look for on a bottle of New Jersey wine: a "seal of approval" that the wines have met or exceeded certain standards.

Think of it this way: You walk into a wine shop and are faced with the tedious choice of choosing *just one* wine. There you'll find over 5,000 wines from California, 1,000 wines from Australia, 900 from Chile, 50 from Washington, and perhaps a few from Oregon, New York, maybe even Bulgaria.

Oh, and a few from New Jersey squeezed in-between.

Now, if you're like most wino aficionado's, you'll go for something that you've had before or something that's been recommended to you. Why? Because of all the "iffy" wines on that shelf, that's why. People tend to go for what they know.

But if these wines had a seal of approval from a governing body which could guarantee you a good bottle of the state's finest wine, would you try it? You'd probably be slightly more inclined to grab that bottle of New Jersey wine and give it a shot.

The NJQWA is modeled after Canada's Vintners Quality Alliance (VQA), which has been very successful in raising the overall quality of the wines. New Jersey's quality program, like the VQA, is voluntary – wineries do not have to participate or submit all of their wines for judging.

Here's how the NJQWA works:

- •Wineries submit all the wines they would like to have evaluated (which may all or just some of the wines they produce).
- •A panel of judges is chosen, having a variety of backgrounds including commercial winemakers, distributors, wine media, liquor store and restaurant owners, as well as trained wine judges and sommeliers.
- •The wines are tasted blindly (so no one knows the wine or its producer) by the panel of judges who score the wine on a simple pass/fail scale. The judges use both objective and subjective criteria, but are mainly looking for obvious flaws in each wine.
- •If the wines pass, they're allowed to put the NJQWA logo on their wines. Generally, you can find the logo on the bottle's neck or imprinted directly on the wine's label.

The NJQWA is the only quality alliance on the East Coast, and is only one of three in the United States. The idea, made famous by Canada's VQA, is a great way to ensure that the wine you buy meets commercial standards. Since its inception, many other states' wine-growing associations have contacted New Jersey's officials for more information on the idea and concept of a quality alliance.

The program is a great way for New Jersey wineries to raise the public's awareness, interest and trust in their wines and in the wine-growing industry as a whole.

Thanks to Dr. Joe Fiola of the Rutgers Cooperative Extension in Cream Ridge for providing information about the NJQWA.

Things to Know Before You Go!
(or, things I learned while writing this book!)

1. Give yourself ample time and don't schedule anything else to do "back home" on the day of your visits. The whole idea of a winery is to lose a sense of time – talk, tour, and try some wine *(and hopefully BUY! BUY! BUY! when you find something you like!!)*. The people who greet you in the winery more than likely either own the wineries or make the wine, so spend some time talking and asking questions. You might even make some new friends.

2. Dress comfortably. None of the wineries are formal. Or even semiformal. Plus, New Jersey is one of those wonderfully diverse states where it can be chilly and drizzly on one end and scorchingly hot on the other. Be prepared for anything.

3. Bring friends and family along. It's much more fun to visit the wineries in small groups. Kids are welcome, too (and some wineries even have fresh grape juice – *free for kids!)*.

4. Don't be afraid to try all the wines. Maybe you only like sweet wines, dry wines, Chardonnays or Niagaras. Maybe you only like diet 7-Up. Even though you may think you only like one type of wine, try all the wines available for tasting – you may find that your tastes have evolved. Keep an open mind. Besides, many wineries offer free tastings (or charge a nominal fee) so it's no loss to you!

5. Take notes. In each chapter I've included only a selection or two from the winery's wine list. The rest is up to you. Don't worry about wine lingo. If a wine smells like pears, pineapples or blackberries, say so. On the flip side, if it tastes like diesel fuel, potting soil, or a wet saddle, say so – you may be on to something! It's not necessary to like every wine tried, but it's a good idea to record your likes and dislikes for future reference. Use the space under the recipes and in the back of the book for your own notes!

6. Bring cash (although most take personal checks and credit cards, too!) to purchase your favorites. You'll probably find something at each winery that grabs your attention. Plus, once you see the reasonable prices of some of New Jersey's wines, you'll be making room in your car's trunk before you even reach for your wallet.

7. Plan on buying at least one bottle of wine at each winery. (*No, I don't work for the wineries.*) That said, most of the wineries covered in this book are small, and they count on tasting room sales to make money. Of course, this is just a suggestion. All of the wineries have wine priced under $10, so I can almost guarantee you'll find something worth buying at each! (*Buying a bottle from each of the wineries is still cheaper than taking a family of 4 to a baseball game, ya know!*)

8. Take advantage of the local attractions. Just because the winery is a little out of the way doesn't mean it's in the middle of nowhere. Call ahead or ask each winery when you arrive for local attraction suggestions. They would be more than happy to do so. Also, if you're touring a couple wineries in one region, make plans to stay at a local B&B for the night or weekend. I've listed a few favorites (*suggested by the wineries and me*) in the "New Jersey Wine Trails" section.

9. Bring your camera. Many of these wineries are located in unbelievably gorgeous settings. Snap some photos as you travel through the region – you'll have memories and some new art to frame!

10. Pace yourself and don't overdo it. If you're going to hit a few wineries in one day, make sure you stop to eat in between, lest you walk into the next winery with blurry eyes. It's always a good idea to pack a picnic lunch, and most wineries have picnic areas where you're free to munch. Enlisting a designated driver is not such a bad idea.

11. ENJOY YOURSELF!!

1. Alba Vineyard
2. Amalthea Cellars
3. Amwell Valley Vineyard
4. Balić Winery
5. Cape May Winery & Vineyard
6. Cream Ridge Winery
7. Four Sisters Winery
8. King's Road Vineyard
9. Marimac Vineyards
10. Poor Richard's Winery
11. Renault Winery
12. Sylvin Farms
13. Tomasello Winery
14. Unionville Vineyards
15. Valenzano Winery

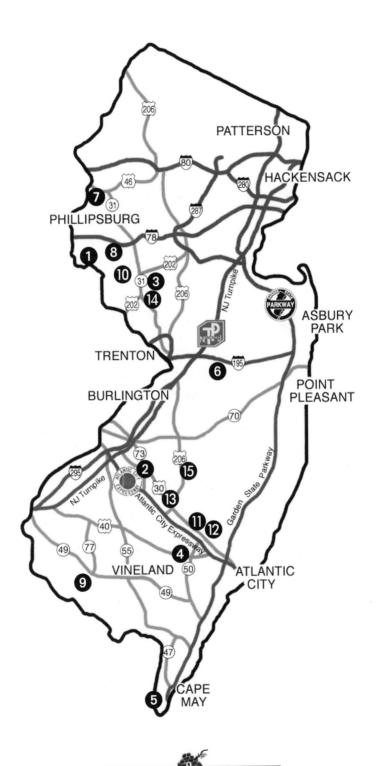

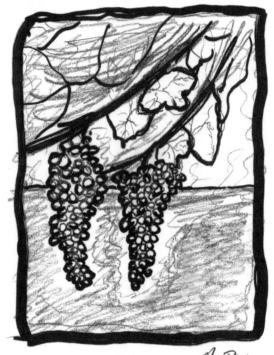

New Jersey Wineries

A barrel of wine
can work more miracles
than a church full of saints.

— Italian Proverb

ALBA VINEYARD

Founded:	1983
Owners:	Rudy Marchesi & Tom Sharko
Winemaker:	Rudy Marchesi
Address:	269 Route 627
	Village of Finesville
	Milford, NJ 08848
Phone:	(908) 995-7800
Fax:	(908) 995-7155
WWW:	www.albavineyard.com
Hours:	Sun, Wed & Thurs 12 – 5 p.m.,
	Fri 12 – 7 p.m., Sat 11 – 6 p.m.
Annual production:	7,000 cases
Price range of wines:	$5.99 – $18.00
Amenities available:	Wheelchair accessible, restrooms, adjoining art gallery.

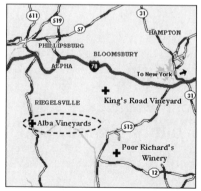

Directions:

From NYC: Take I-78 west to exit 7 (Bloomsbury). Bear right off ramp onto 173 west. When the road forks – bear left toward Riegelsville, onto 639 west. Follow 639 to stop sign. Bear left onto 519 south. Continue straight: road will turn into 627 south, winery is on the right.

From Philadelphia: Take the Blue Route to exit 27 (Willow Grove.) Take 611 north into Riegelsville. Turn right at the light and follow signs to business district. Bear right after Baby Brooklyn, then straight onto 627 north. The winery is on the left.

No matter which way you come via route 627, you're bound to see some wonderful scenery. Once arriving at the winery, you're in store for even more.

Alba Vineyard, open since 1983, is now home to the Musconetcong Fine Art Gallery. Along with festivals and concerts throughout the summer, Alba hosts local artists, exhibiting their work on the walls of the winery.

Rudy Marchesi, winemaker and co-owner of Alba, has high aspirations for the winery. "We want to be a cultural center for the

Alba's beautiful historic barn houses the winery, tasting room and art gallery.

community," he says, making the classic connection between wine and art.

"We consider what we do a high craft," says Rudy, proud of what Alba's become. "Sometimes we meet the art form."

Rudy's art is created in the cellar, which was built with limestone walls and set into the hillside to keep it a perfect temperature for winemaking. Inside you'll see stacks of new oak barrels and large stainless steel tanks filled with soon-to-be award-winning wines.

"We're not trying to be somebody else – we're trying to find out who we are," asserts Rudy, noting that he's traveled the world's vine-yards and each has its own style and flair.

Rudy has guided Alba to find a style of its own using grape varieties that grow best in the region.

Rudy uses Marechal Foch in a number of his wines. "It's a great grape," he proclaims. Taste his vintage port and you'll agree. This rich, intense, chocolately wine is 100% Foch.

Alba Vineyard is also the East Coast home of Windsor Vineyard, a California-based winery that leases space from Alba. Windsor sells its wines in the tasting room, but that's the extent of their relationship – no grape or wine sharing between them.

One of Alba's many strong points is its creative use of the historic barn built on the site in 1805. The barn houses the tasting room, art gallery and winemaking facilities. It has been preserved and is in great shape. As you tour the winery, notice the old stone and wooden beams that still support the barn.

*U*niquities:

- *Winery housed in historic barn, circa 1805.*
- *Musconetcong Gallery, which adjoins the winery, displays local art for sale.*

Another of Alba's perks is the Musconetcong Gallery, where you can view the wares of local artists. Take a tour of the wonderful art – all of which is for sale – while enjoying the masterpiece in your glass!

Wine Selections:

Heritage: Hearty red blend of Foch and Cabernet Franc. Smooth and drinkable now, but should age well.

Port: Exquisite!...and getting better every year. Flavors of dark cherries and chocolate swirl in your mouth – all from Foch grapes.

*R*ecipe

Chocolate Almond Cake a la Alba

Cake Ingredients:
4 oz semisweet chocolate, chopped
1/4 cup unsweetened butter
1/2 cup blanched almonds
2/3 cup sugar (divided)
3 tbsp cornstarch
3 eggs, separated
4 tbsp Alba Red Raspberry Wine
1/4 tbsp cream of tartar

Frosting Ingredients:
3/4 cup whipping cream, chilled
1 1/2 tsp sugar
1 1/2 tsp Alba Red Raspberry Wine
1/2 oz semisweet chocolate, grated

Cake: Position rack in the center of the oven; preheat to 350 degrees. Butter a 9 x 1 1/2-inch round cake pan. Line the bottom with parchment or foil; butter lightly. Melt chocolate and butter in a large heat-proof bowl set in a pan of hot water over low heat; stir until smooth. Then, cool for about 10 minutes.

Grind nuts with 3 tbsp of the sugar in a food processor until as smooth as possible, then transfer to a small bowl. Thoroughly mix in 4 tbsp sugar and the cornstarch. Stir into chocolate. Beat in egg yolks with a wooden spoon until mixture is smooth and thick. Stir in wine.

Using clean beaters, beat egg whites with cream of tartar in a large bowl until soft peaks form. Beat in remaining 1/4 cup of sugar, 1 tbsp at a time. Continue beating until whites are stiff but not dry. Fold one-third of the whites into the chocolate mixture to lighten it. Spoon chocolate mixture back into whites; fold until blended and no white streaks remain. Pour batter into prepared pan.

Bake about 25 minutes. Let cool for 10 minutes, then run a thin-bladed knife around sides of the cake. Carefully turn out onto a wire rack and remove paper. Invert and cool completely. Refrigerate at least one hour before frosting.

Frosting: Beat cream with sugar and wine in a chilled bowl until soft peaks form. Spread on the sides and top of the cake. Grate chocolate on top. Serve at room temperature.

Serve with Alba Vineyard Red Raspberry Wine.

(This recipe was submitted by Alba Vineyard.)

AMALTHEA CELLARS

Founded:	1985
Owners:	Louis Caracciolo
Winemaker:	Louis Caracciolo
Address:	209 Vineyard Road
	Atco, NJ 08004
Phone:	(856) 768-8585
Fax:	(856) 753-1099
Hours:	Saturday & Sunday 11 a.m. – 5 p.m.
Annual production:	3,000 cases
Price range of wines:	$6.50 – $21.99
Amenities available:	Wheelchair accessible, restrooms, banquet facilities, picnicking.

Directions:

From Philadelphia: South on Black Horse Pike (Rte. 168). Left on Evesham Road. Turn right onto White Horse Pike (U.S. Rte. 30). Turn right onto Vineyard Road. Just after the lake – you'll see the sign for the winery. Winery is on the right.

From New York City: NJ Turnpike south to route 73. Follow south until round-about and take second exit onto Milford Road. Then, take South White Horse Pike (U.S. Rte. 30) and turn right onto Vineyard Road. Winery is on the right.

In 1981, just as the winery was being bonded, the twelfth moon of Jupiter was discovered and named Amalthea. It was described as being the size of New Jersey, so the winery's owners thought it only appropriate to name the winery in honor of the new moon.

Since then, owner Lou Caracciolo has built an expansive, yet modest operation over the years. The main building that welcomes your arrival houses a sales area, a tasting room, the wine cellar and the Caracciolo's home. Next door, there's a guest house with dining as well as banquet and wedding facilities.

Lou is a food scientist and an inventor. He has an affinity for unique – some ancient – patented items. In the tasting room, the wines are opened with an odd, but incredibly efficient corkscrew patented in the 1800s.

But, it's his training as a food scientist that plays a deep role in his winemaking. Lou is an international wine and food consultant – giving him access to the

You'll find some exquisite red wines inside Amalthea Cellars.

minds and experiences of some of the greatest winemakers in the world.

He's no doubt used this advantage to make some superior wines. In the cellar, Lou is blending his reds in the styles of France's great winemakers.

"I'll release them as 'Legend's Edition' wines, mimicking the greats," says Lou.

Of course, it's all in the grape growing and the process of winemaking, not so much in the winemaker, Lou says, modestly. He believes that the more you "do" to a wine, the more you chip away at its final outcome. "I'm just the custodian of the natural process," says Lou. With this in mind, don't expect to find heavily filtered, processed wines at Amalthea.

What you will find are a hearty variety of wines, ranging from dry to semi-dry. Most are varietal wines – Cabernet Sauvignon and Pinot Noir, Chardonnay and Riesling. Lou breathes new life into the Chancellor variety, giving it character rarely found in this wine.

*U*niquities:

- **Great Chancellor and Bordeaux blend red wines.**
- **Rustic winery building with unique tasting room and gift area.**

To meet demands for two styles of Chardonnay, both California (bolder fruit) and French (more subtle, *sur lie*) styles are presented and they're each very distinct.

But it's the blended wines that have unique names you may not recognize. The semi-dry Metis and the dry white Elara Blanc, as well as any other blended wines produced by Amalthea, are named after other moons of Jupiter.

Continuing with this theme, the winery is adorned with a variety of wind chimes, candles, scales, and astrological symbols. From the moment you enter the sales area, you'll feel the personal, if not planetary touch given to the winery by its owners.

Wine Selections:

Elara Blanc: interesting blend of Chardonnay and Riesling.
Chardonnay: two styles, both very good – one oaked, *sur lie.*
Chancellor Reserve: Amalthea's older vintages are aging well – expect soft tannins and ripe fruit.

*R*ecipe

Dunph's Baked Ziti

Ingredients:

2 tbsp olive oil

1 box cut ziti

3 cups of spaghetti sauce

1 egg

4 cloved garlic, pressed

fresh parsley, chopped

1 – 3/4 oz ricotta cheese

2 cups shredded mozzarella

6 cups water

salt and pepper to taste

1 tbsp butter or margarine

dash of oregano

Heat oven to 375. Bring 6 cups water and olive oil to a boil. Add ziti and bring to a boil again and stir occasionally for 9 minutes.

In an extremely large bowl, mix egg, garlic, oregano, parsley, ricotta cheese, salt, pepper, half the jar of spaghetti sauce, and 1 and one half cup mozzarella cheese. After draining ziti, add butter to colander and mix throughout. Add ziti to other mixture and mix until all ingredients are combined. Place into a 9 x 13 glass baking dish (ungreased). Add remaining sauce to the top of the ziti and then add the remaining mozzarella cheese on top of that. Cover with foil. Bake for 25-30 minutes; cheese should be melted and sauce bubbly.

Serve with Amalthea Cellars Elara Blanc.

(This recipe was submitted by Alicia Dunphy of Avon-by-the-Sea, NJ.)

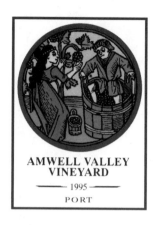

AMWELL VALLEY VINEYARD

Founded:	1982
Owners:	Dr. Michael Fisher, Jeff & Debra Fisher
Winemaker:	Jeff Fisher
Address:	80 Old York Road
	Ringoes, NJ 08551
Phone:	(908) 788-5852
Fax:	(908) 788-1030
WWW:	www.amwellvalleyvineyard.com
Hours:	Sat & Sun 1 - 5 p.m., other times by appt.
Annual production:	1,700 cases
Price range of wines:	$7.00 – $20.00
Amenities available:	Restrooms, wheelchair accessible, banquet and wedding facilities.

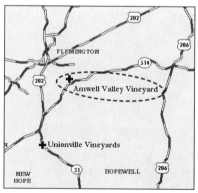

Directions:

From NYC: Take the NJ Turnpike south to exit 14. Take I-78 west for 25 miles to I-287 south toward Somerville. Then, U.S. Route 202/206 south to 514 (Reaville exit). Follow 514 (Old York Rd) to the winery on your right.

From Philadelphia: Take I-95 north across Scudder Falls Bridge to New Jersey. Take first exit, 29 north (at end of bridge) toward Lambertville. Go north on U.S. Route 202 to 514 (Reaville exit). Follow 514 (Old York Rd) to the winery on your right.

"It used to be that when someone pulled into the property the entire family would walk up to greet you," says winemaker Jeff Fisher, noting that when the winery started, not many people were adventurous enough to try New Jersey wines.

Take a turn off route 514 onto the Fisher's property nowadays and you'll be greeted by rows of Foch grapes – a welcoming sight nonetheless.

Pull up a stool and taste the many wines of Amwell Valley Vineyard.

Much of the state's wine history lies in the Fisher's own history. Under Dr. Michael Fisher, Jeff's father, Amwell Valley Vineyards was the first winery to be licensed under the Farm Winery Act which Dr. Fisher who helped get the legislation passed in 1981.

Then, Fisher was instrumental in beginning the Hunterdon Wine Growers which eventually evolved into the Garden State Wine Growers Association.

A lot has changed since then: Jeff and Debra have assumed the day-to-day operations at the winery. Jeff mans the vineyard and winemaking portions of the work, and Debra takes care of the retail business.

Nobody ever said this job was easy – romantic, maybe – but not easy. "You could start losing your mind after a while," said Jeff. Good thing the Fishers hired their first full-time employee in 1999. Scott Gares had just the right mix of vineyard and winery experience to be the perfect match for Amwell.

Jeff still works in the vineyard, though not as much as he used to. "Bending down is still the hardest part!" Jeff says.

If you want a tour, make sure you check out Amwell's banquet room and deck overlooking the vineyard. With its view, its sound system and full bar, it's the perfectly romantic – and practical – location for a wedding.

The vineyard seems to be in the best possible location: it's planted on a south-facing, gentle sloping hill just below the winery. The 30 acres are neatly planted with hybrid varieties like Seyval, Foch, Landot Noir, Aurora, and Vignoles. *Vinifera* like Riesling, Chardonnay, Cabernet Sauvignon, and Gewurz-traminer are also in the lineup.

*U*niquities:

- *Extensive line-up of wines.*
- *Perfect facilities for both banquets and weddings – overlooking vineyards and rolling hills.*

There's still some room on the land, and the Fishers plan to add Cabernet Franc to the vineyard soon.

More than 15 wines are produced by Amwell Valley Vineyard, including some sparkling. The modern tasting room is bright and includes another great view of the vineyard. Behind the tasting bar, you'll see the Fisher's collection of corkscrews, which should inspire you to taste some of Amwell Valley's fine wine.

Wine Selections:

Chardonnay: Oak-aged yet still light and fruity, with crisp, apple flavors filling the palate.

Aurora: Semi-sweet white wine with an almost cult-like following.

Landot Noir: Aged in American oak and created in the Beaujolais style, this medium-bodied red is fruity and ready for drinking.

*R*ecipe

Amwell Valley's Potivagel

Ingredients:
One large eggplant
One small onion chopped
1/2 red pepper, chopped
1/4 cup extra virgin olive oil
2 tablespoons wine vinegar
salt and pepper to taste

Place whole eggplant on a baking sheet. Broil, rotating once, until eggplant skin crackles and fork slides easily into eggplant (which can also be grilled!) Remove eggplant from oven, chop ends off and remove skin carefully – it will be hot! Chop eggplant or use food processor until eggplant is smooth. Add other ingredients and serve on a crusty loaf of French bread.

Serve with Amwell Valley Vineyard's Landot Noir.

(This recipe was submitted by Debra Fisher of Amwell Valley Vineyard.)

BALIĆ
WINERY

Founded:	1974
Owners:	Balić Inc.
Winemaker:	Savo Balić
Address:	U.S. Route. 40, Box 6623
	Mays Landing, NJ 08330
Phone:	(609) 625-2166
Hours:	9:30 a.m. to 5:00 p.m. Monday – Saturday
Annual production:	17,000 cases
Price range of wines:	$6.65 – $11.95
Amenities available:	Wheelchair accessible, restroom.

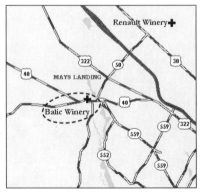

Directions:

From Atlantic City and South: Take U.S. Route 322/40 west and follow route 40 into Mays Landing. The winery will be on your right just after the intersection with route 50. Look for the big green sign.

From Philadelphia & East: Take U.S. Route 40 east to Mays Landing. The winery will be on your left. Look for the big green sign.

On the way to Atlantic City on U.S. Route 40, it's hard to miss the big green sign announcing Balic. If the sign doesn't catch your attention, the multitude of American flags will.

Once inside this seemingly patriotic house, you'll be greeted by a thick accent...a slavic accent. Owner Savo Balić is outgoing and will make you feel at home at once! He has a knack for subtle humor and enjoys interacting with his guests.

Savo was born an American but was raised in a European winery. He jokes about how his grandfather used to pick him up and put him in a tub to crush grapes. Growing up around grapes and wine certainly had its advantages, though. When Savo returned to the United States, he was comfortable enough with winemaking to

Balić Winery's large green sign is hard to miss when driving on U.S. Route. 40.

open Balić Winery.

The entire winery is housed in the solitary, pale, cinderblock building. The tasting room is usually filled with relaxing classical music, which enhances your visit, allowing you to relax and prepare for tasting Balić's wine.

The long, arching tasting bar sits atop a wood-paneled base and is large enough to accommodate all of Balić's wines and a good many guests, too.

When it comes time to taste, you'll notice the reasonable prices. Some of the wines are worth far more than their $6 - 7. So, why so cheap?

"I don't want to get rich," says Savo, "I just want to make a living."

Most of Balic's grapes come from the vineyards that surround the winery on three sides. These grapes, primarily hybrid varieties, are planted on Balic's 30 acres of land.

These vines help to produce Balic's 12-15 wines of all varieties. There are some unique tastes and styles here, but a guest summed it up best.

"They have sweet, dry and fizzy wines," he says, making it clear that there's something here to please everyone.

In fact, it seems like everyone has found a favorite. Mays Landing locals make frequent stops to pick up their "house wines" from Balic, as do tourists on their way to the shore.

*U*niquities:

- *Owners provide a great mix of humor, history and fine blended and varietal wine.*
- *Some great sweet and semi-sweet blends.*

So, is Balic so patriotic that he needs to have six American flags waving outside the winery? Yes! But, you have to admit, the flags really draw people in.

Once inside, you can't help but to enjoy Savo Balic's charm, witty comments, and inexpensive, quality wine.

Wine Selections:

Blush: Sweet but meaty enough to serve with dinner.
Chenin Blanc: Dry, crisp and fruity. A great match with fresh fish.
Classic White: Nice balance of spicy acidity and some sweetness.

Magic Cookie Bars

Ingredients:
1/2 cup butter
1 1/2 cup graham cracker crumbs
14 oz can sweetened condensed milk
6 oz pkg, chocolate morsels
3 1/2 can coconut (1 1/2 cup)
1 cup chopped nuts

Preheat the oven to 350 degrees or 325 degrees if you're using a glass dish. In a 13x9 dish, melt the butter in the preheated oven. Sprinkle graham cracker crumbs over butter. Mix this and press down.

Pour milk over the crumbs and top with remaining ingredients (layer of chocolate morsels, then coconut). Press top down firmly. Bake for 25-35 minutes or until coconut is lightly browned.

Serve with Balić Winery's Blush for the perfect snack!

(This recipe was submitted by Balic Winery.)

CAPE MAY
WINERY & VINEYARD

Founded:	1995
Owners:	Joan and Bill Hayes
Winemaker:	Bill Hayes
Address:	709 Townbank Road
	Cape May, NJ 08204
Phone:	(609) 884-1169
Fax:	(609) 884-5131
WWW/E-mail:	www.capemaywinery.com
Hours:	By appointment only (new tasting room
	opens in 2001 with regular hours)
Annual production:	1,000 cases
Price range of wines:	$8.00 – $20.00
Amenities available:	Restroom, wheelchair accessible.

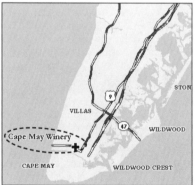

Directions:

From the North: Take the Garden State Parkway south to route 109 west then turn left onto route 9 south. Turn right onto Seashore Road and turn left at the light onto Townbank Road. The winery is on the right.

From Cape May Ferry: Take route 9 north. Turn left at the second light onto 644. Turn right onto 648 at next light. Winery is on the left.

A few years back, Bill and Joan Hayes realized that with all Cape May had to offer, the town was missing one thing: a winery.

"There were many great restaurants and B&Bs, but no wineries," says Bill. If they had any doubts before, all were washed away during the first summer season when they sold out of most of their wines before September. They've increased production since, and still their supply dwindles by the end of summer. About ninety percent of Cape May's wine is sold through restaurants during the summer months.

"I can't make enough wine to satisfy people," says Bill.

As the summer tourist season heats up, thousands of cars pass by the winery each weekend. Located just outside the town's business district, the winery's five acres are dense with mature vines – many

Cape May Winery is perfectly located just minutes from downtown Cape May.

of which, like Cabernet and Merlot, were thought not to flourish in this region.

Then came Bill's meeting with Gary Pavlis and Joe Fiola from Rutgers. "We tested the site and it looked great!" says Bill. The vineyard is currently planted with Chardonnay, Cabernet Sauvignon, Cabernet Franc, Merlot and Riesling.

Bill was also heavily influenced by Frank Salek from Sylvin Farms Winery. Salek's encouragement persuaded Bill to jump from home winemaker to small commercial winery. "I worked with him for years – for one or more days a week," says Bill, who says he learned most of his skills from Salek.

"If I make good wine, it's because of Frank Salek," says Bill.

Bill will need this knowledge when all of his vineyards are finally planted and in production. Another six and a half acres, located just down the road, will be planted over the next few years.

"The demand is for white wines during the summer," says Bill. And that's what he's planting – more Chardonnay, some Viognier and perhaps even some Sauvignon Blanc and Pinot Grigio.

*U*niquities:

- *Right at the tip of NJ in the heart of Cape May.*
- *Great barrel-aged vinifera red wines – at very reasonable prices!*

Since most of the wine is sold through retail stores in Cape May restaurants, there hasn't been a need for a public tasting room. But now, with increased production, the Hayes have added an addition to their home that will become their new tasting room. Until it opens in mid-2001, you're more than welcome to call and set up an appointment to purchase wine.

"I'm the winemaker, pruner and bottlewasher," says Bill, describing his duties as home-winemaker gone commercial. Joan works in the vineyard, but also in the office doing the accounting and computer work. "She's the vice president, secretary and so on," Bill says admiringly.

Wine Selections:

Victorian Blush: The cure for summer's heat; light and refreshing.
Merlot: This is a lot of wine for such a small amount!
Cabernet Sauvignon: Heavy tannins, full body and ready to age!

Godmother's Veal Megan

Ingredients:
6 oz veal medallions pounded to 1/8 inch thick
2 tbsp butter
1 tbsp flour
3/4 cup Cape May Winery's Reserve Chardonnay
1/2 medium ripe tomato cut 3/4 inch dice
4-5 medium sea scallops
4 medium shrimp peeled and deveined
3 tbsp butter (not melted)
1/8 cup crab meat
pinch of fresh basil
salt and pepper to taste
1/2 lemon

Heat pan on low heat and add butter. Cook the veal and remove from pan. Add flour and mix well, raising the heat to medium. Then, add the Reserve Chardonnay and mix well.

Add tomatoes, basil and scallops and cook until scallops are almost done. Then add the shrimp, 3 tbsp butter and crab meat: cook thoroughly. Add cooked veal and squeeze in 1/2 lemon through a strainer.

Finally, add salt and pepper to taste, and serve over angel hair pasta!

Serve with Cape May Winery's Reserve Chardonnay

(This recipe was submitted by Godmother's Restaurant in Cape May.)

CREAM RIDGE WINERY

Founded:	1988
Owners:	Thomas Amabile
Winemaker:	Thomas Amabile
Address:	145 Route 539
	Cream Ridge, NJ 08514
Phone:	(609) 259-9797
Fax:	(609) 259-1852
www:	www.creamridgewinery.com
Hours:	Monday thru Saturday 11 a.m. to 6 p.m.,
	Sunday 11 a.m. to 5 p.m.
Annual production:	5,000 cases
Price range of wines:	$6.95 – $18.95
Amenities available:	Wheelchair accessible, restrooms.

Directions:

From the NJ Turnpike: Get off at exit 7A. Bear to the right on to I-195 east. Take route 539 south to Allentown. After crossing the bridge, 539 makes a sharp left onto High Street. Look for the winery on the right.

From the East and Shore Points: Take I-195 west toward Trenton, and take exit 16 onto route 537 west. Turn right at the first light onto to route 539 north toward Allentown. Look for the winery on the left.

If you're visiting the winery via Interstate 195, you'll meander through quaint Allentown. Keep on turning, and eventually you'll see it: the big red barn with "WINERY" written on it. If this announcement doesn't entice you inside, you're a lost cause!

Once inside, you'll be surrounded by gifts, gourmet jellies and sauces, and, of course, wine. The Amabile family owns and operates the winery, and you're sure to be greeted by at least one of them while you're there.

"Every wine is a challenge," says Tom Amabile, Cream Ridge's proprietor and winemaker. He's been making wine for over 30 years. And it shows, because so many of Cream Ridge's wines have great

Always busy, Cream Ridge Winery is a favorite stop for shore-goers throughout the year.

character and flavors. The winery excels in its line-up of fruit wines, for which it's famous. In addition, Cream Ridge is making some respectable hybrid and *vinifera* wines as well.

"In 2000 we won our third Governor's Cup for our cherry wine," says Tom. "Ciliegia Amabile," as it's called, is a sweet wine made from Montmorency cherries that tastes like pie. The name makes the wine even more special – Ciliegia means "cherry" in Italian, and while Amabile is the family name, it also means "slightly sweet" in

Italian. Either way, this wine's great alone or added to dessert recipes – it's a hit no matter how you enjoy it!

Some of Cream Ridge's fruit wine offerings include Cranberry, Rhubarb, Apricot, Red Raspberry, and Aurelio, made from nectarines and peaches!

But don't stop there. Cream Ridge offers 23 wines: eight of them fruit wines and the others ranging from Chardonnay to "A Perfect Blend," a blend of Cabernet Sauvignon, Cabernet Franc and Merlot aged in oak.

Amabile blends grapes and other fruit together to make some of his wines. Raley's Red, a dry blend of grapes and berries, is a wonderful match to spaghetti and other Italian dishes, all while retaining the fruity finish that has made Cream Ridge so popular.

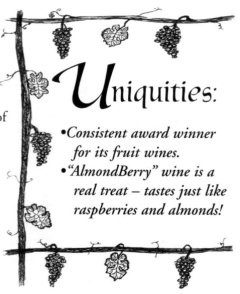

Uniquities:

- *Consistent award winner for its fruit wines.*
- *"AlmondBerry" wine is a real treat – tastes just like raspberries and almonds!*

The winery is also well-known for hosting unique events like its Fruit Crush and Pig Roast Festival in October and annual bluegrass festival. These are always fun events and they're in a great setting.

"I can't think of any business as good as this," says Tom. You'll agree, and once you try Cream Ridge's award-winning wines, you're sure to return.

Wine Selections:

AlmondBerry: The best seller! Raspberries and white wine create this nutty, sweet treat.

Ciliegia Amabile: In Italian, "sweet cherry"… and it's a multiple award winner.

Grandma's Cheese Cake

Ingredients:
1 cup sugar
2 tbsp flour
1/4 tsp salt
2 large packages cream cheese
1 tsp vanilla
5 eggs separated
1 cup heavy cream (1/2 pint)
graham cracker crust (ready made – or you can make your own)

Mix sugar, flour, salt and cream cheese. Add vanilla and yolks of eggs and beat. Add cream and mix again. Beat egg whites until they peak. Fold into the cream cheese mixture. Pour mixture into springform pan already containing a graham cracker crust. Bake 325-350 degrees for 1 hour or until center is set.

Serve with Cream Ridge Ciliegia Amabile.

(This recipe was submitted by Cream Ridge Winery.)

Four Sisters Winery

Merrill Blush
Semi-dry Rosé Table Wine
Produced & Bottled by Four Sisters Winery • Belvidere, N.J.
B.W. #272 • Alcohol 11% by Vol.

FOUR SISTERS WINERY

Founded:	1984
Owners:	Robert & Laurie Matarazzo
Winemaker:	Robert Matarazzo
Address:	10 Doe Hollow Lane, Route 519
	Belvidere, NJ 07823
Phone:	(908) 475-3671
Fax:	(908) 475-3555
www:	www.matarazzo.com/winery.html
Hours:	March thru December, all week 9 a.m. - 6 p.m.
	January & February, closed Wednesdays
Annual production:	7,600 cases
Price range of wines:	$7.95 – $12.95
Amenities available:	Wheelchair accessible, picnic table, restrooms,
	Matarazzo Farms market open Sept. - Oct.

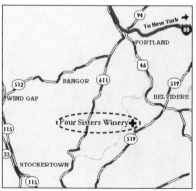

Directions:

From New York City: Take I-280 west to I-80 west. Take route 521 exit, turn left at the fork in the ramp and continue onto 521. Stay on this road for 5 miles until it becomes route 519. Winery will be on the right. Look for Matarazzo Farms.

From the South: Take I-476 north to route 22 east. Take route 57 east toward Washington, then turn left on Uniontown Road. Make a slight right onto Upper Belvidere Road. Turn right onto South Bridgeville Road (519) and look for the winery on the left.

For years, Matty (Robert) and Laurie Matarazzo had made quite a business growing, harvesting and selling their farm-fresh produce at Matarazzo Farms in Belvidere. Then in 1984, a new product hit their market: wine. Lots of wine. The Matarazzos opened Four Sisters Winery in a building adjoining the already well-known Matarazzo Farms.

Four Sisters is known regionally for its unique and unusual events. Matty says the events are more than just about attracting people to the winery.

"I try to incorporate agricultural and historical aspects of the region into the festivals," says Matty. One such event is an expedition that takes customers out onto the property to find morel mushrooms. Then, they'll meet back at the winery where a chef will pre-

Since Four Sisters Winery is attached to Matarazzo Farms, fine wine and fresh produce are yours for the picking.

pare their loot. Another example is the "Return to Beaver Creek Native American Indian Festival" complete with traditional food, music, song and dancing.

Matty spent a few years consulting fruit growers in Sonoma County, California, a region known around the world for its quality grapes and wine. He feels that while Sonoma generally produces high quality wine, New Jersey wineries produce wines for all different palates. And as Matty says, "You can't say that about Sonoma."

Matty spends most of his time amidst the various crops his family produces. If he's not at the winery, chances are he's out in the vineyard or on the tractor, making sure all crops are progressing as they should.

But the vineyard has not been without its traumas. In the winter of 1994-95, the region was pummeled by temperatures sinking to -14 degrees Fahrenheit. While some of the vines were devastated, one variety, Leon Millot, survived unscathed.

"This variety thrives on stress," Matty says. He's been able to make a complex, full-bodied wine from this red varietal. "The quality of the fruit is unbelievable," says Matty, hardly believing the vines survived at all.

If you're a do-it-yourselfer, Matarazzo Farms offers "pick your own" raspberries, strawberries, apples, pumpkins and Concord grapes (in season, of course).

Uniquities:

- *Unusual events – always fun with an informative & educational spin!*
- *Adjoins Matarazzo Farms fresh produce market.*

And, in case you're wondering, there really are four sisters. Melissa, Serena, Robin and Sadie Matarazzo have provided Matty and Laurie with endless inspiration. In addition to a winery named in their honor, wines are dedicated to each of them. To top that off, the wines are labeled with a beautiful painting of the four Matarazzo daughters, the original of which hangs in the winery above the tasting bar.

Wine Selections:

Cayuga: Meaty yet fresh, a great match with chicken.

Leon Millot Reserve: Estate bottled, intensely flavored, dry red; good choice with seasoned dishes.

Harvest Apple Chicken & Rice

Ingredients:
2 tbsp margarine or butter
4 boneless, skinless chicken breast halves (about 1 lb)
1 package (6 oz) Rice-A-Roni Herb Roasted Chicken
1/2 cup Four Sisters' Sadie's Apple wine
1/2 cup apple juice
1 medium apple, chopped (about 1 cup)
1 cup sliced mushrooms
1/2 cup chopped onion
1/4 cup dried cranberries or raisins

In large skillet over medium-high heat, melt 1 tbsp margarine. Add chicken; cook 2 minutes per side or until brown. Remove from skillet and set aside. In the same skillet, sauté rice mix according to directions on the package, using remaining 1 tbsp margarine.

Add 1-1/4 cups water, apple juice, Four Sisters' Sadie's Apple wine, chicken, apple, mushrooms, onion, cranberries and special seasonings. Bring to a boil.

Cover, and reduce heat to medium-low. Simmer for 15-20 minutes or until chicken is cooked through and rice is tender. Let stand 5 minutes before serving.

Serve with Four Sisters' Sadie's Apple wine.

(This recipe was submitted by Four Sisters Winery.)

KING'S ROAD
VINEYARD

Founded:	1980
Owners:	KRV Inc.
Winemaker:	Nicolaas Opdam
Address:	360 Route 579
	Asbury, NJ 08802-1231
Phone:	(800) 479-6479, (908) 479-6611
Fax:	(908) 479-1366
www:	www.kingsroad.com
Hours:	Wednesday - Sunday 12 to 5 p.m.
	Tours on weekends from April through October
Annual production:	17,500 cases
Price range of wines:	$5.70 – $18.00
Amenities available:	Restrooms, picnic area.

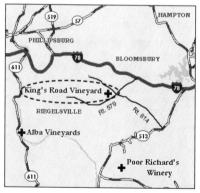

Directions:

From NY: Take the GW Bridge to I-95 south. Continue to I-78 west to exit 11. Bear left following signs for Pattenburg. You will go over I-78 heading south. The road becomes route 614. Follow 614 about three miles to route 579. Turn right onto 579, winery is on the left.

From Trenton: Take route 31 north to Ringoes. Continue on U.S. Route 30 202/31 into Flemington and follow route 31 to I-78. Follow I-78 west to exit 11. Follow directions above to winery.

When you approach the winery, you'll see King's Road Vineyard nestled in the valley on the left. Surrounded on three sides by vineyards, this is one of the state's most scenic wineries.

From the outside, the main building seems very new, but once inside you'll begin to see its long history. Notice the huge old, dark beams crossing the ceiling in the foyer and tasting room.

The building is a converted dairy barn and the tasting room is actually built in what used to be a hay loft. These massive beams still provide the building's main support.

Nicolaas and Lorraine Opdam joined the winery in 1991, and under their direction, much renovation has occurred to the winery building as well as innovation in the vineyard.

Upon arrival to this area, the couple traversed New Jersey, visiting the local wineries and decided that King's Road would depart from what they thought was the region's common "characteristic and style."

This couple left King's Road Vineyard with two cases of wine!

To do this, they began in the vineyard, retraining the vines in a way that would increase both yield and quality employing a combination of successful methods used in the United States and abroad.

So well traveled and versed in fine wine, Nick Opdam's influence can immediately be tasted in King's Road's wine. As winemaker, he wants his wines to reflect the quality of his grapes, so he uses French and American oak barrels for his premium reds and Chardonnay, some of which are left to age undisturbed for years.

In addition to longer aging of his wines, Nick has introduced ultra-modern computer-controlled fermentation and storage cellars. King's Road's modern facility helps him to produce consistent, quality wines.

The vineyard, which takes great advantage of the property's ideal slope, is impeccably maintained. The exact rows of vines are pruned tightly in the early spring and both Nick and Lorraine carefully tend to the vines throughout the growing season.

Since they believe the quality of the wine begins on the vine, they take every precaution to ensure the grapes are harvested at their peak maturity with an automatic harvester, which greatly saves on time and labor.

Now, on to the wine. This is some of New Jersey's finest *vinifera* wine, yet it's still very affordable. Nick prides himself on creating top-quality Chardonnay, Cabernet Sauvignon and the elusive Pinot Noir.

*U*niquities:

- *Some of the best **vinifera** wines in New Jersey!*
- *Winery and tasting room are in a restored dairy barn.*
- *Beautiful site for picnicking.*

The Opdams view wine competitions as not only an accomplishment but as a challenge to maintain strict standards. Judging by the many medals and awards displayed in the tasting room, King's Road plays to win.

Wine Selections:

Chardonnay Reserve: Aged strictly in French oak, this is one of New Jersey's great whites!

Marcato: Semi-dry red blend of Cabernet and Merlot. Very smooth, versatile wine – it matches well with most dishes.

ecipe

Red Wine Pot Roast

Ingredients:
3-4 lb beef pot roast
1 small onion, chopped
3/4 oz. packet of dry beef gravy mix
1 cup water
1/4 cup ketchup
1/4 cup King's Road Marcato (dry red table wine)
2 tsp Worcestershire sauce
2 cloves garlic, minced
2 tsp Dijon mustard
salt and pepper to taste

Sprinkle roast with salt and pepper and place it in a slow cooker (crock pot). Mix remaining ingredients in a small bowl and pour over roast. Cook for 8-10 hours on low setting.

It's easy, makes the house smell so good, and it's delicious, too!

Serve with King's Road Vineyard Marcato.

(This recipe was submitted by King's Road Vineyard.)

MARIMAC
VINEYARDS

Founded:	1998
Owners:	Clarence McCormick Sr., Marie, Kevin, Clarence Jr., J. Brent McCormick, Bill Emenheiser
Winemaker:	Bill Emenheiser
Address:	65 Marimac Road
	Bridgeton, NJ 08302
Phone:	(856) 459-1111
www:	www.marimacvineyard.com
Hours:	Saturdays 10 a.m. to 3 p.m., or by appointment.
Annual production:	800 cases
Price range of wines:	$13.00 – $14.00

Directions:

From Philadelphia: Take U.S. Route 322 east to route 45 south. Follow to route 77 south. to route 49. Go west on route 49 and make a left on Fayette Street. Follow straight to the end.

From the Shore: Take route 49 west to Bridgeton. At the fourth traffic light, turn left onto Fayette Street. Follow straight to the end.

It started the way these things typically do. Amateur winemaker Bill Emenheiser was looking for a place to plant vines to feed his hobby when someone suggested property on the Cohansey River. He planted some test vines and they grew vigorously – almost too vigorously. Soon, the hobby was officially out of control.

"We're not an aggressive business – we're a grown-up hobby," jokes Bill, who says he and the other owners have yet to place ads, distribute wines or do many of the "businessy" things that wineries sometimes do. Plus, there's little need to push the wine, since, as Bill says, it's flying off the shelves already.

"We haven't been marketing because the wine's been disappearing so quickly," says Bill, who manages the winemaking while his part-

Marimac's beautiful vineyard slopes gracefully down toward the Cohansey River.

ners take care of the other important business. Brent McCormick manages the vineyard while Clarence McCormick Jr. and his brother Kevin McCormick take care of sales and marketing.

Marimac grows mostly vinifera varieties, including Pinot Gris, Riesling, Chardonnay, Cabernet Sauvignon, and Cabernet Franc. Chambourcin makes the lineup as the only hybrid in the vineyard. And due to the region's moderate microclimate, these vines – some of which struggle throughout most of the rest of New Jersey – are excelling at Marimac.

As for the wines, Bill makes them in a dry style, including an interesting dry blush made from the original "test" rows of grapes he planted in 1992. They're a superb example of the utmost quality that New Jersey wineries can produce given the right location and craftsmanship.

If the initial reaction to Marimac's wines is any prediction of its future success, they're already well on their way. With their first full vintage, Marimac wines won four medals, including a gold and bronze medals for the 1998 Chambourcin Reserve and a bronze for the 1998 Cabernet Sauvignon.

The wine cellar is in what would have been the McCormicks' tractor garage. From the outside, the winery looks like a nondescript home, strangely missing a front door. The entrance to the winery is down around back through one of three large retractable garage doors.

*U*niquities:

- *One of the newest wineries in the state.*
- *Award-winning* **vinifera** *wines since the first vintage in 1998!*

"We may put a tasting room upstairs with a front entrance," explains Bill, although no definite plans have yet to be made.

Sometimes Bill thinks he's crazy for letting his hobby get out of hand. "I have no idea why I'm doing this," Bill says, laughing. Once you try his award-winning wines, you'll surely do your part to keep him in business.

Wine Selections:

Chardonnay: Moderately oaked and medium-bodied.

Chambourcin: Gold-medal winner! Nice and full with moderate tannins and a bit of spice.

Baked Salmon Marimac

Ingredients (serves four):
four salmon steaks
olive oil
lemon pepper
parmesan cheese

Preheat oven to 350 degrees F.

Dredge salmon in olive oil and cover both sides with a liberal coat of lemon pepper and dust with Parmesan cheese.

Coat the bottom of the pan with a light coat of oil as well. Bake for 20-25 minutes or until the fish flakes.

Suggested serving mates: fresh bread, garden salad, boiled new red potatoes.

Serve with Marimac Vineyards Dry Riesling.

(This recipe was submitted by the staff of Woodbury Vineyards.)

POOR RICHARD'S WINERY

Founded:	1990
Owners:	Richard Dilts & Judy Rampel
Winemaker:	Richard Dilts
Address:	220 Ridge Road
	Frenchtown, NJ 08825
Phone:	(908) 996-6480, (908) 806-6468
www:	www.intac.com/~poorrich
Hours:	Saturday & Sunday 12 to 5 p.m.
	Weekdays by appointment only.
	January through March by appointment only.
Annual production:	1,000 cases
Price range of wines:	$6.35 – $10.00
Amenities available:	Picnic/event deck atop winery, restroom.

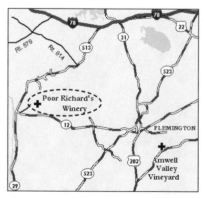

Directions:

From I-78: Take exit 15, then south on route 513 to Frenchtown, then left onto route 12, then make your third left onto Ridge Road. Winery is on your right.

From Flemington: Take route 12 west, at the second traffic light turn right onto route 519, turn left onto Ridge Road. Go 1.5 miles and make a left into the winery.

From I-95: Take route 29 north to Frenchtown, then take a right onto route 12, then make your third left onto Ridge Road. Winery is on your right.

When visiting Poor Richard's Winery, you get the feeling you're in the middle of nowhere. Just minutes out of Frenchtown, you find yourself perched atop a hill so high, your view of the valley stretches for miles. You'll pass vineyards on your left as you drive down the unpaved road to the winery.

At the bottom of the hill you're greeted by a deck with "Poor Richard's" inscribed on its fence. The actual winecellar and tasting room sit discreetly beneath the deck, submerged below ground. This keeps the cellar at an ideal temperature even during the summer months.

While the facilities may be modest in comparison to some other

Richard Dilts is the winemaker and chief bottlewasher for Poor Richard's Winery in Frenchtown.

regional wineries, the wines are up to par, having won medals in just about every competition they're entered.

"Welcome," says winemaker and co-owner Richard Dilts, as he greets guests of his winery. Next, you'll probably meet Grizzly, the resident cat. Inside the winery you'll find a strange mix of bottles, barrels, tanks and a tasting bar. The main attraction, of course, is the tasting bar where you can try all of Poor Richard's ten wines.

"Our main line is hybrids," says Richard who makes everything from a barrel-fermented Seyval to a Reserve Red – a combination of Chambourcin and Chancellor.

The on-site vineyard provides most of Poor Richard's grapes, although they do buy some from local growers. Estate-grown grapes include Leon Millot, Chancellor, Chambourcin, Vidal and Seyval. Richard says the vineyards at the top of the hill will eventually be trimmed down or replanted completely, but for now the ten acres in production are adequate.

Richard is an old-pro in the business. He's been making wine since the early '70s and has made his business out of solid, quality wines.

"If we didn't have good wines, we couldn't be in business," he says, pouring a taste of his Reserve Red. He's right, it's very good. And not at all overpriced. All of Poor Richard's wines are inexpensive, with the reserve wines topping out at only $10-12.

*U*niquities:

- *Winery is set in a hillside with an deck atop its roof where you can enjoy the scenery and the wines!*
- *Great Vineyard Red Reserve.*

If you like the wines, buy them while you're at the winery because they're not for sale in retail shops or restaurants. "We sell direct to the consumer – no middleman," Richard says, proudly. He feels customers should not have to pay extra to get good wine, plus he most definitely enjoys the company!

Wine Selections:

Terra Rosada: Very good semi-dry blush; perfect complement to a light snack or meal, or enjoy it on its own!

Chancellor: Very light, easy-drinking wine with low tannins.

Vineyard Red Reserve: Surprisingly bold, yet balanced half & half blend of Chancellor and Chambourcin.

Widow McCrea's Famous French Toast

Batter Ingredients:
1 quart eggnog
3 tbsp cinnamon
1 tsp clove
1 tsp nutmeg
1 tsp apple pie spice
2 tsp Frangelica

Topping Ingredients:
1 lb fresh or frozen strawberries
1/3 cup sugar
3 tbsp Grand Marnier

And of course:
thick slices of challah bread

Combine and whisk ingredients into a batter. Then, soak the bread in the mixture and refrigerate overnight.

Sprinkle sugar over the strawberries and refrigerate overnight. In the morning, add the Grand Marnier. Let stand for 30 minutes at room temperature.

Sear both sides of the bread in a non-stick pan. Pre-heat oven to 450 degrees and bake bread on a cookie sheet for ten minutes.

Serve with a combination of the warmed straberry topping and maple syrup.

This recipe makes for a fine meal at any hour of the day. And if you're enjoying this meal at a "suitable" time, pair this french toast with a glass of Poor Richard's Terra Rosada.

(This recipe was submitted by Widow McCrea House in Frenchtown, NJ.)

BLUEBERRY FLAVORED
American Champagne
CHARMAT BULK PROCESS
Naturally Fermented - Sparkling Wine

RENAULT
WINERY

Founded:	1864
Owners:	Joseph Milza
Winemaker:	Fernando Valesquez
Address:	72 N. Bremen Avenue
	Egg Harbor City, NJ 08213
Phone:	(609) 965-2111
Fax:	(609) 965-1847
WWW:	www.renaultwinery.com
Hours:	Tours & tastings all week 11 - 4 p.m.
	Restaurant serves dinner Fri and Sat 5:00 to 8:30 p.m.;
	Sunday 4:30 to 7:30 p.m.
Annual production:	33,700 cases
Price range of wines:	$7.99 – $19.99
Amenities available:	Wheelchair accessible, full-service restaurant,
	restrooms, banquet and wedding facilities.

Directions:

From Philadelphia: Take Atlantic City Expressway to the Egg Harbor exit (17). Turn left onto route 50 north, turn right onto U.S. Route 30. Turn left onto Bremen Avenue, 2 1/4 miles to the winery on the right.

From North Jersey: Garden State Parkway south to exit 44. Sharp right onto Moss Mill Road (Alt. 561), follow five miles to Bremen Avenue. Turn right and follow to winery.

"When I first visited the winery, I was amazed; the soul was here but the body was falling apart," says Renault Winery owner Joe Milza, who bought the operation in 1977.

What he found was a property at the end of its era – worn by years of production and activity. His Milza's wealth of ideas and entrepreneurial spirit have guided the winery into the next era.

Renault is the oldest winery in the state and the oldest estate-grown vineyard and winery in the United States.

So much about this winery is romantic. Even from the parking lot, the ponds, bridges, geese and statue fountains take you into another time, one with much more grace and elegance than that found in the towns and on the highways that brought you here.

Renault is so much more than just a winery. This courtyard is just one of the the winery's diverse settings.

Once inside the Renault complex, you'll begin to see just why it's so popular. You could easily get lost in the twists and turns of the many hallways, but all of them lead to the heart of the winery.

The wine cellars are immense, housing large stainless steel tanks and oak barrels enough to produce 40,000 cases of wine! There's a grand ballroom with a stage large enough to host local opera productions with an elegant lobby picture perfect for weddings.

Upstairs is a restaurant with a wrap-around bar that serves wines and wine cocktails (no beer or liquor served here!). And keeping with the wine theme, there are even cask (wine barrels, not coffins...) booths where you can enjoy the utmost privacy during your meal. Standard entrées include herb-roasted filet mignon, honey mustard glazed roast rack of lamb and potato encrusted mahi mahi. But, to top it off, dinner is all-inclusive – six courses are served with tastings of two wines, although with six courses you may need to sample a few more wines.

When you visit the winery, be sure to request a tour with Richard Higgins. He's a historian, humorist, and quite the tour guide.

Richard's been on board at Renault since 1984 and with all that experience, he will lead you through the step-by-step process of wine-making as you waltz through the tiled and arbored halls of Renault Winery. The tour ends at the tasting bar where you and 40 of your closest tourmates can acquaint yourself with Renault's 24 wines.

*U*niquities:

- *Oldest winery in New Jersey.*
- *It's becoming a full-service resort complete with a golf course, hotel, banquet, meeting and wedding facilities.*

Milza and his supporting staff have created a monumental winery. . . but they're not done yet. Future additions include a 102-room hotel complex directly across Bremen Avenue that will house a restaurant, banquet facilities and a golf shop. Why a golf shop? To support the new golf course which will be added by 2001.

Wine Selections:

Pink Lady: This popular sweet blush easily takes the edge off summer.
Merlot: Dry and mellow with low tannins – a perfect pasta wine.
Blueberry Champagne: Semi-sweet and pleasantly effervescent!

*R*ecipe

Skillet Seared Rabbit Tenderloin *(or Chicken Breast)* on a Sweet Potato Clementine Gravy

Ingredients for gravy:

1 carrot, diced
1 medium onion, diced
4 sweet potatoes, diced
1 cup duck (or similar) fat
4 cups rabbit or chicken stock
3/4 tbsp rosemary, chopped
1/2 tbsp sage, chopped
4 cloves garlic

1 tbsp dry mustard
1 clementine, quartered
1 cup apple cider
5 clove
1 tsp cayenne pepper
salt & pepper to taste
1 cup brown sugar

Place all ingredients – except stock, sugar and apple cider – in a large sauce pan. Place on a high heat and cover, stirring occasionally. When vegetables become slightly tender, add stock, juice and brown sugar. Bring to a boil and then lower heat to a simmer and let cook for 20 minutes uncovered. Remove pan from flame and pour into a china cap (or similar strainer). Take a ladle and press vegetable mixture through china cap until all the juice is extracted. Place gravy on serving plate and set rabbit or chicken on top, garnish and serve.

Ingredients for preparing meat:

8 rabbit tenderloins
   or chicken breasts
3 tbsp sage, chopped

3 tbsp rosemary, chopped
3 tbsp oil
salt & pepper to taste

Heat skillet and crust the rabbit or chicken with herbs. Drizzle the skillet lightly with oil and sear the rabbit or chicken for about 3 minutes on each side. Remove from skillet and serve with gravy on top.

Serve with Renault Chardonnay.

(This recipe was submitted by the the chefs of Renault Winery.)

SYLVIN FARMS

Founded:	1977
Owners:	Dr. Frank Salek
Winemaker:	Dr. Frank Salek
Address:	24 N. Vienna Avenue
	Germania, NJ 08215
Phone:	(609) 965-1548, (973) 778-1494
Fax:	(973) 778-9165
Hours:	Weekends, by appointment.
Annual production:	1,300 cases
Price range of wines:	$6.00 – $18.00
Amenities available:	Wheelchair accessible, restroom.

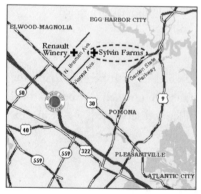

Directions:

From Philadelphia: Take Atlantic City Expressway to the Egg Harbor exit 17. Turn left onto route 50 North, turn right onto U.S. Route 30. Turn left onto Vienna Avenue, 2 1/2 miles to the winery on the right.

From North Jersey: Garden State Parkway south to exit 44. Sharp right onto Moss Mill Road (Alt. 561), follow four miles to Vienna Avenue. Turn right onto Vienna Avenue, 1/2 mile to winery.

Just when you thought you were lost, vineyards appear along with a sign announcing Sylvin Farms. And what a welcome sight it is.

Owner and winemaker Frank Salek is a man who enjoys an enormous reputation. Maybe it's his attention to detail. Perhaps it's the way he thinks about winemaking and grape growing. Or it could be the advice he gives to those wanting to join the wine industry.

"The easiest way you can get someone to fail in this business is to encourage them to do it in the first place," says Salek with a mischievous grin. Then again, maybe it's his keen sense of humor that's created his celebrity.

"The first wine you make is the best wine you make… even if it's undrinkable," Salek says, although he admits his skills have much improved since the days when he learned winemaking from his father-in-law.

Frank's passion outgrew the basement and he and his wife Sylvia bought the property on which Sylvin Farms now resides.

When the winery opened in 1977, the Saleks commuted from their North Jersey home – some 120 miles away – twice or more weekly. They had always been planning to

Dr. Frank Salek does it all – and he does it well.

retire and make the move to the winery.

With Sylvia's untimely death in 1999, Frank has assumed the reins and is continuing with plans to relocate to the winery permanently upon retirement from his professorship at the Newark College of Engineering, where he's taught for over 30 years.

Salek makes only traditional *vinifera* wines. His wines have won the Governor's Cup in the state wine competition six times, and he's continually awarded compliments by customers, wine writers and his winemaking peers.

But they're not the only ones who like his wine.

"I could drink all of my Blanc de Noirs," he says, breaking a smile after taking a sip. "They go so well with everything." As do the rest of his wines, his conversation, and his overwhelming amount of knowledge on the topic of winegrowing.

Out in Sylvin Farms' seven acres of vineyards, you'll find Cabernet Sauvignon, Cabernet Franc, Pinot Noir, Chardonnay, Riesling, Merlot and others. New plantings of Syrah and Viognier *(with even more on the way)* exemplify Salek's adventurous expansion. But he says the winery will grow only as large as he alone can handle.

Frank Salek is a master at what he does. He has been for years, and still remains a driving force in the state's indus-

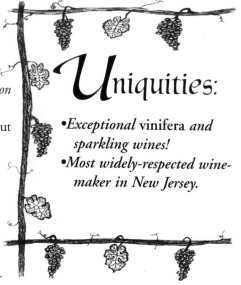

*U*niquities:

- *Exceptional* vinifera *and sparkling wines!*
- *Most widely-respected wine-maker in New Jersey.*

try, encouraging newcomers by giving them honest advice and sharing his many experiences.

He realizes that the state's wineries are not competing with each other, but rather with the rest of the world's wines. And he's confident that if the wineries work together, they'll excel.

"I think we can produce some very good wines," says Salek of the New Jersey wineries, "in fact, I know we do."

Wine Selections:

Blanc de Noirs: Perfectly balanced sparkling wine, worth so much more than the asking price!

Cabernet Franc: Barrel-aged with soft tannins. Drink now or cellar.

Hot Ricotta Spinach Loaf de DeManss

Ingredients:
1 refrigerated pizza crust dough
1 pkg. frozen chopped spinach, thawed & drained
8 oz of ricotta cheese
1/4 cup of banana peppers, chopped
1/2 cup grated parmesan or romano cheese
1 tbsp olive oil
8 oz marinara sauce

Unroll pizza crust dough on a 12- by 15-inch baking sheet. Mix ricotta cheese, spinach, banana peppers, parmesan or romano cheese and spread mixture evenly over the dough.

Starting at a long edge of dough roll to enclose filling. Set the loaf, seam down, on baking sheet. Brush loaf top with olive oil.

Bake in a 425 degree oven until well browned, 12-15 minutes. Meanwhile, stir marinara sauce in a 1-1/2 quart pan cooking over medium heat until hot.

Slice loaf diagonally, making 10 equal portions. Drizzle some marinara sauce over loaf and pop back into the oven for 3-5 minutes.

Can be served as an appetizer or as a hot sandwich.

Serve with Sylvin Farms Blanc de Noirs or Pinot Grigio.

(This recipe was submitted by Mary DeManss, assistant editor of the book.)

TOMASELLO WINERY

Founded:	1933
Owners:	Charles and Jack Tomasello
Winemakers:	Charles and Jack Tomasello
Address:	225 North White Horse Pike
	Hammonton, NJ 08037
Phone:	(609) 561-0567, 1-800-MMM-WINE
Fax:	(609) 561-8617
www:	www.tomasellowinery.com,
Hours:	Monday - Saturday 9 a.m. to 6 p.m.
	Sunday 11 a.m. to 6 p.m.
Annual production:	40,000 cases
Price range of wines:	$6.00 – $24.00
Amenities available:	Wheelchair accessible, banquet facilities for rent, restrooms.

Directions:

From Philadelphia: Take the Atlantic City Expressway to the route 54 exit. Turn left and follow to U.S. Route 30 and turn right. Winery is on the left.

From Atlantic City and East: Take A. C. Expressway west for 30 miles to route 54. Take 54 north to U.S. Route 30. Turn right and the winery is on the left.

From the North: Follow NJ Turnpike south to exit 7. Take U.S. Route 206 south to U.S. Route 30. Turn right and the winery is on the right.

Some kids never leave home. Others take over. As is the tradition in the Tomasello family, brothers Charlie and Jack Tomasello have continued to grow the family business. Tomasello Winery's third-generation winemakers, Charlie and Jack, had the challenge of expanding an already prosperous family business.

When Frank Tomasello, Charlie and Jack's grandfather, founded the winery in 1933, he had no idea how popular his family's wines would become. Reviewed regularly in the *New York Times*, Tomasello's wines have become a standard by which other local wines are judged.

In addition to being so popular around town, Tomasello wines are exported – most notably the Blueberry Wine, which is sold in

Guests at Tomasello Winery are faced with an enormous challenge: "Where do I start?"

Japan and Malaysia, where wine lovers can't seem to find enough!

When you visit the mediterranean-styled winery, you'll always be greeted by friendly staff. The bright tasting room is finely decorated with original art with a large wine rack behind the tasting bar showcasing Tomasello's many wines. Step up to the bar and you'll be faced with some difficult decisions. Tomasello has more than 30 wines available at any given time, and most are available for tasting. Plus, the wines cover a spectrum of styles and tastes: dry, sweet, fruity, tannic, smooth, sparkling – you name it, they've got it. You can't help but to find a few to take home with you.

Tomasello grows much of its own grapes and maintains 70 acres of vineyards in Atlantic County. Other grapes are bought from both in and out-of-state sources to fill the more than 40,000 cases of wine they make every year.

While there are no official tours of the winery, you can walk around back to see the neatly kept vineyards, or take a peek into the banquet hall used for special events. "The Vintner's Room," as it's called, is perfectly suited for a wedding – there's an alcove with a tall ceiling and marbled flooring making it truly romantic.

Reigning as New Jersey's largest winery, Tomasello has been a leader in marketing its wine and advancing the state's wine industry as a whole. Comparable in size to many of California's most famous wineries, Tomasello produces over 50 percent of New Jersey's total wine production!

*U*niquities:

- *Largest winery in NJ, producing over 30 wines.*
- *Blueberry wine is famous here and in their largest export region – Asia!*

With this in mind, it's well worth spending an afternoon (or even the whole day) trying Tomasello's wine list of over 30 wines, exploring the immense production facilities, or just taking respite in this haven located just off busy White Horse Pike.

Wine Selections:

Chardonnay Oak Reserve: Rich and buttery, aged in oak for 7 months.
Sparkling Rkatziteli: Made in conjunction with Sylvin Farms. It's semi-sweet and makes for a beautiful after-dinner sparkler.

Tomasello's Veal Framboise for Two

Ingredients:
8 oz of veal medallions (flatten with a mallet)
1 1/2 oz of butter
1/2 cup of flour
1 tbsp of finely chopped shallots
4 - 6 oz of Tomasello Red Raspberry Wine
4 - 6 oz of Tomasello Chardonnay
4 - 6 oz of heavy cream

In a sauté pan, melt one ounce of butter (clarified is preferable). Flour the veal medallions and sauté on both sides until brown. Set aside in a covered dish.

Remove any excess grease from the pan. De-glaze the pan by adding equal portions (4 - 6 oz. each) of Tomasello Red Raspberry Wine, Tomasello Chardonnay and the finely chopped shallots. Reduce to approximately 1/3 of the original volume. Add the cream and again reduce to half over low flame. Salt and pepper to taste. Finish with 1 ounce of butter and return veal to pan.

Serve with Tomasello Oak Reserve Chardonnay.

(This recipe was submitted by Tomasello Winery.)

UNIONVILLE VINEYARDS

Founded:	1993
Owners:	Kris Nielsen and Patricia Galloway
Winemaker:	John Altmaier
Address:	9 Rocktown Road (P.O. Box 104)
	Ringoes, NJ 08551
Phone:	(908) 788-0400
Fax:	(908) 806-4692
www:	www.unionvillevineyards.com
Hours:	Thursday thru Sunday 11 a.m. - 4 p.m.
Annual production:	5,000 cases
Price range of wines:	$6.99 - $21.99
Amenities available:	Restrooms, picnic tables.

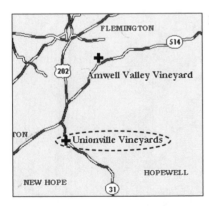

Directions:

From NYC: Take the NJ Turnpike south to exit 14. Take I-78 west to I-287 south. Then, take U.S. Route 202/206 south. Take jug handle onto Wertsville Road in Ringoes. Turn right onto Rocktown Road, and the winery is on the left.

From Philadelphia: Take I-95 north across Scudder Falls Bridge to New Jersey. Take route 29 north toward Lambertville. Go north on U.S. Route 202 for six miles. Turn right on Wertsville Road and follow to Rocktown Road. Turn right and the winery is on the left.

As you drive up the long gravel drive, you're provided with a quick glimpse of history. Ahead sits a stately manor house which used to overlook a peach orchard, and now a vineyard. The large, red barn that houses the winery has been around since the mid-1800s, and originally served as a dairy barn.

Presently, the barn proudly serves as the home of Unionville Vineyards, often referred to as New Jersey's best winery by the *New York Times* and other outlets. Perhaps that's because its wines have won more than 200 medals since its first vintage was released in 1993. Or maybe it's because of the overall quality and character of the wines.

After climbing the steps up to the entrance, you'll be greeted by a friendly staff and a beautiful tasting room. Inside, the barn retains

Unionville Vineyard's winery and tasting room are almost as impressive as its wines.

some of its original character, while allowing modern accommodations. Century-old wood beams still provide the main support for the building.

The tasting room overlooks the winery's main cellars and production areas by way of a large pane of glass. Looking through this window is like peeking into the kitchen of a fine restaurant: you can actually *see* the barrels and tanks where the wine in your glass was produced.

But, rather than smudging the glass, ask for a tour if you want to check out the cellars. Under the tasting "loft" is a barrel cave used for private tastings.

"We're really committed to the vines here," says winemaker John Altmaier, *Vineyard and Winery Management* magazine's 1998 wine-maker of the year. Although Altmaier works mostly in the winery, he believes in the value of quality vineyards. Almost 80 percent of Unionville's wines are estate grown – a true feat given the breadth of the operation. The winery also works with grape growers in South Jersey allowing them to select other quality Jersey-grown fruit.

The wines are divided into three distinct labels. The Hunter Series consists of French hybrid varieties like Cayuga, Chambourcin and Vidal. The Windfall Series is comprised of wines from another of Unionville's vineyards, including Seyval Blanc and Riesling varietal wines. And finally, the Traditional Vinifera series is reserved for Unionville's premium noble varieties such as Chardonnay and Cabernet Sauvignon.

*U*niquities:

- *Beautiful tasting room in a restored barn – with a wall of glass looking into the cellars.*
- *Very high-quality wines.*

In addition to the craftsmanship that molds the wines, many of the labels are works of art, including original paintings by a local artist Jeff Echevarria. The Hunter's White Reserve garners a different one of Echevarria's paintings each year.

Don't pass up on a visit to Unionville Vineyards – the superb wine and the overall experience should not be missed.

Wine Selections:

Riesling: Real crisp, semi-dry. Easily matched with food.
Chambourcin: Very smooth with forward fruit.

Unionville's Hunter's Gold Winter Wine

Ingredients:
1 bottle Unionville Vineyards Hunter's Gold Apple Wine
2 cinnamon sticks
3 cloves
2 tbsp sugar

Heat ingredients in a crockpot or simmer in a pot on the stove top until sugar is dissolved. The longer and more slowly the wine simmers, the more the flavors develop!

(This recipe was submitted by Unionville Vineyards.)

VALENZANO WINERY

Founded:	1998
Owners:	Anthony Valenzano, Anthony B. Valenzano, and Mark Valenzano
Winemaker:	Anthony B. Valenzano
Address:	340 Forked Neck Road
	Shamong, NJ 08088
Phone:	(609) 268-6731
Fax:	(609) 859-8014
www:	www.valenzanowine.com
Hours:	By appt only. Call before going – someone's usually there 7 days a week.
Annual production:	4,200 cases
Price range of wines:	$6.90 – $9.50
Amenities available:	Wheelchair accessible, restroom.

Directions:

From Philadelphia: Take I-295 north to route 70 east. Follow to U.S. Route 206 south and turn left on Forked Neck Road and the winery is on the right.

From the North: Follow NJ Turnpike south to exit 7. Take U.S. Route 206 south to Forked Neck Road. Turn left and the winery is on the right.

From Atlantic City: Take A.C. Expressway west to route 54 north. Follow to U.S. Route 206 north to Forked Neck Road. Turn right and the winery is on the right.

Don't be fooled into thinking the winery's never open just because it has no formal tasting room hours. "By appointment only" is the Valenzano family's way of saying "just stop by."

"We live on site, so if someone pulls in and wants wine, we'll sell it to them!" says Anthony Jr., winemaker and general partner in the winery. He says that while someone's always around, it's still best to call first, just in case.

There are a host of reasons to visit Valenzano. First, it's very new. Some of the grapes have been in the ground since 1995, but the winery's only been open since 1998. In these few years, Valenzano has expanded from just two wines to over ten at any given time.

Valenzano Winery is located at the end of the driveway, just behind the Valenzano's home in Shamong.

Anthony Jr. admits he learned the winemaking craft simply from reading and from trial and error. More trials than error, it seems, because Valenzano's wines have been a great success at festivals and in their retail stores. But the trials continue on...with new styles and varieties of wine.

One of Valenzano's newest wines, Cynthiana, is attracting attention and is part of a growing revival for this grape variety. The grape has been a cult favorite in the midwest for decades, selling for upwards of $30. Just recently "rediscovered" by winemakers on the East Coast, Cynthiana – also known as Norton – is being hailed as the next great red wine. Noted for its low tannins and dark red (almost purple at times) color, this wine is superb with just about anything off the grill.

Even though Valenzano has only been open since 1998, it has already added onto the winery. The building is a rambling structure that winds around and everything seems to be spread out comfortably.

"I don't like to lift anything, so everything's all around – no ups and downs," says Anthony, explaining the outward expansion. This expansion was not just for convenience. Even in the first year of production, space quickly disappeared and the winery needed to grow.

*U*niquities:

- *Only winery in NJ to grow/produce a wine from the Cynthiana grape.*
- *All wines are under $10. Get 'em while they last!*

"We're finally at the point where we've got everything where we need it," says Anthony Jr., pointing to the new bottling line. But they'll keep on growing as long as there's such a demand for their wine.

The Valenzano's just planted 20 acres of Cynthiana, Cabernet Franc, Vidal Blanc and Chambourcin at a new site near the winery, which will be coming on line in the next few years.

Call first, but do stop by Valenzano Winery – with an empty trunk to fill with their many under-$10 wines.

Wine Selections:

Shamong Red: Made from Concord, it's semi-sweet and robust.
Cynthiana: This red wine is sure to be a long-term success! Its very bold fruit flavors and deep color are amazing,
Blueberry: Like drinking a bowl of blueberries.

Mama's Spaghetti and Clams

Ingredients:

1 tbsp olive oil

2 cloves garlic

1 can of stewed tomatoes

8 oz of tomato sauce

2 – 6.5 oz cans of clams

Sauté the crushed garlic in olive oil. Add stewed tomatoes and tomato sauce. Add the juice from the canned clams. Simmer for about 15 minutes until sauce thickens. Add the clams to the sauce and simmer for a few more minutes. Pour sauce over your favorite pasta and top with chopped fresh parsley and grated parmesan cheese.

Serve with Valenzano Red Chambourcin.

Chef Kelly's Cranberry Wine Reduction Sauce

Ingredients:

1 – 750ml bottle of Valenzano
     Winery's Cranberry Wine

4 cups red wine vinegar

2 tbsp sugar

1/2 cup shallots

1/4 lb butter

1 pint heavy cream

In a sauté pan add shallots, Valenzano's Cranberry Wine, and vinegar. Bring to boil and add sugar. Reduce about 90 percent. Take off heat and strain into saucepan, discarding shallots. Add butter and heavy cream. Mix on low heat. Add a touch of garlic, and oregano. Add salt and pepper to taste. Serve over sliced turkey breast with stuffing, sweet potatoes and cranberry sauce.

Serve with a chilled bottle of Valenzano Cranberry Wine.

(These recipes were submitted by Valenzano Winery.)

Up-and-Coming Wineries

While traversing New Jersey's wine regions, I met many people who wish they had wineries of their own. Some will get only as far as dreaming, while others have already applied for licenses and are already breaking ground on their wineries.

These are the folks who will have their own chapter in this book's next edition. They're the wineries you may well be visiting in the near future. I say "may" because opening a winery takes years of planning, dedication and good old-fashioned manual labor.

In this section, only one soon-to-be winery is showcased – not because the others I encountered weren't dedicated, but because they're still in the crucial planning stages where just about anything could happen.

Many unexpected things could pop up, preventing a winery from opening on time, and rather than "exposing" these not-yet-open wineries to countless hoards of winery-hunters (like myself) who show up out of the blue craving wine, they'll be included in the next edition of the book.

So, good luck to all of those wineries-in-planning. And best of luck to this one, who's almost there...

Bellview Winery in Landisville, NJ

Jim Quarella is no stranger to the land. He's a fourth-generation farmer, and it shows in his many vegetable and other crops – and now in his vineyard. "Quality is what keeps you in the business," Quarella says.

The winery is being constructed on a homestead estate circa 1914, on the same property as Quarella's locally famous Bellview

Farms. He plans to open his 10,000-gallon winery in early 2001. Much of the vineyard has already been planted, and more vines will be going in over the next few years. Cabernet Sauvignon, Chambourcin, Lemberger, Shiraz, Chardonnay, Sauvignon Blanc, Vidal, Viognier, and some *labruscas* will round out Bellview's eventual wine list.

Bellview is already licensed and is ready to open "any time now," claims Quarella, who's excited about receiving his winery's first customers as soon as possible.

Bellview Winery's vineyard is flourishing – a good sign of things to come.

If you're passing through Buena, or visiting Balic just 15 miles east in Mays Landing, stop by Bellview Winery to see if they're open to the public yet. If not – be patient, and be ready, because when Bellview Winery finally does open, you'll be one of the first to try the Garden State's newest wine.

BELLVIEW WINERY
150 Atlantic St.
Landisville, NJ 08326
(856) 697-3078

Directions:
From U.S. Route 40: Go north on Central Avenue and right on Atlantic St. Winery is on the right.

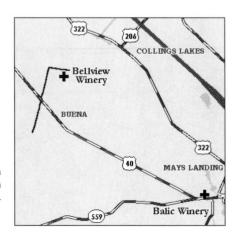

Wine Trails & Regional Suggestions

*Drinking good wine with good food
in good company is one of
life's most civilized pleasures..*

— Michael Broadbent

New Jersey Wine Trails

Let's face it: New Jersey's a very long state. To get to all the wineries in one trip, you'd essentially have to drive from Cape May at the very bottom of the state to Belvidere in the northwesternmost tip. This trip could average you well over four hours (not to mention additional time for traffic)!

If you intend to visit all of the wineries, it's best to break them into manageable chunks – a few at a time in one region, and then a few more in another. The easiest way to divide the state's wineries is into geographic regions.

Northwestern New Jersey Wine Trail

There are six wineries in the northwestern – north and northeast of Trenton – part of the state. These wineries share similar growing conditions and the terrain of this region ranges from hilly to mountainous.

1.	Alba Vineyard	8.	King's Road Vineyard
3.	Amwell Valley Vineyard	10.	Poor Richard's Winery
7.	Four Sisters Winery	14.	Unionville Vineyards

Central New Jersey Wine Trail

In the central portion of the state you'll find Cream Ridge Winery, the sole winery in this region. This trail will be expanding in the coming years as new wineries emerge.

6.   Cream Ridge Winery

Southern New Jersey Wine Trail

Four wineries sit inland, right on or very near U.S. Route 30. This trail can be divided in two to fill an exciting weekend wine trip.

2.	Amalthea Cellars	11.	Renault Winery
4.	Balić Winery	12.	Sylvin Farms
5.	Cape May Winery	13.	Tomasello Winery
9.	Marimac Vineyards	15.	Valenzano Winery

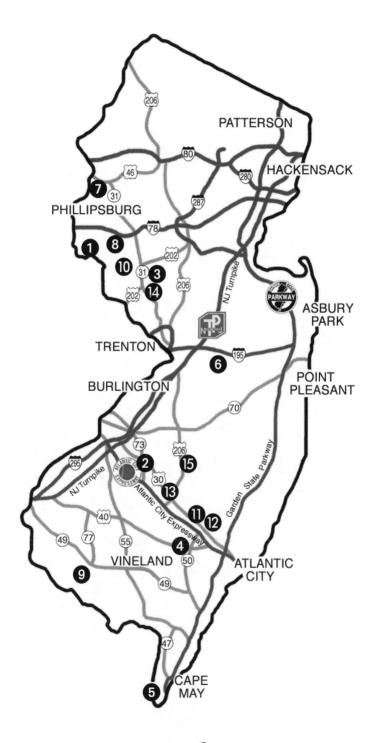

Northwestern New Jersey Wine Trail

This region is quite a nice change of scenery from the Pine Barrens, farms and shorelines of the central and southern portions of the state. The lush forests and sometimes steep rolling hills of northwest Jersey create the perfect scene for vineyards – and a great place to vacation.

In this region, all six wineries are vastly different, so its well worth visiting them all.

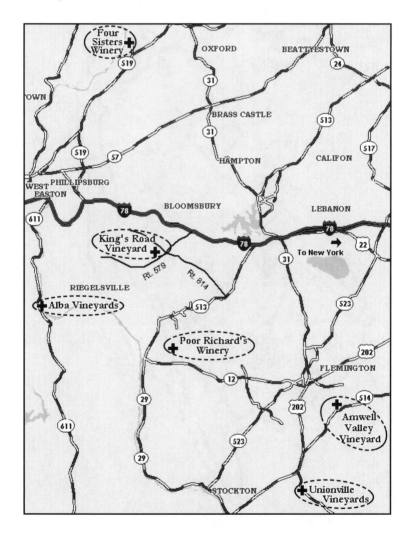

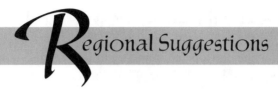

*R*egional Suggestions

Restaurants:

Il Mulino
32 Fulper Rd.
Flemington, NJ 08822
(908) 806-0595

Mountain View Chalet
154 State Rte. 173
Asbury, NJ 08802
(908) 735-4660

La Casa Bianca
326 Main St.
Whitehouse Station, NJ 08889
(908) 534-8384

Muddler Minow
51 Main St. # 49
Clinton, NJ 08809
(908) 730-7782

Mangia Bene
Klines Ct.
Lambertville, NJ 08530
(609) 397-6767

Rosaluca's
1114 Rte. 173
Asbury, NJ 08802
(908) 238-0018

Accommodations:

Cabbage Rose Inn
162 Main St.
Flemington, NJ 08822
908-788-0247

Main Street Manor
194 Main St.
Flemington, NJ 08822
(908) 782-4928

Inn at Millrace Pond
313 Johnsonburg Rd.
Hope, NJ 07844
(908) 459-4884

Stewart Inn
708 S. Main St.
Stewartsville, NJ 08886
(908) 479-6060

Jerica Hill B&B
96 Broad St.
Flemington, NJ 08822
(908) 782-8234

Widow McCrea House
53 Kingwood Ave.
Frenchtown, NJ 08825
(908) 996-4999

Ma Maison Inn
44 Coryell St.
Lambertville, NJ 08530
(609) 397-8292

Woolverton Inn
6 Woolverton Rd.
Stockton, NJ 08559
(609) 397-0802

Central New Jersey Wine Trail

Currently, the only operating winery in the "central" portion of the state is Cream Ridge Winery. When including Cream Ridge in your wine itinerary, you can take advantage its proximity to the southernmost wineries on the northwestern wine trail.

The two closest wineries to Cream Ridge are Unionville and Amwell Valley – only an hour and a half away (and only minutes apart from each other). There are tons of things to do along the I-195 corridor near Cream Ridge Winery, including Six Flags Great Adventure, outlet shopping, and of course, you're only 45 minutes from the shore!

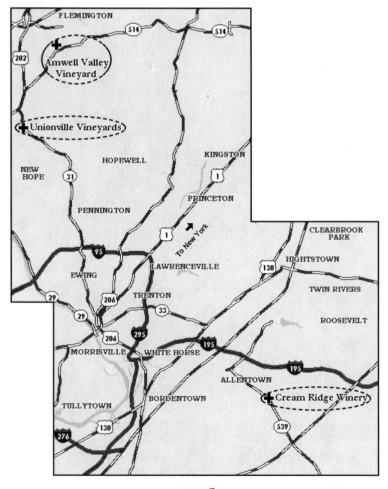

egional Suggestions

Restaurants:

Black Forest Restaurant
42 S. Main St.
Allentown, NJ 08501
(609) 259-3197

Happy Apple
Rte. 526
Imlaystown, NJ 08526
(609) 259-7889

Accommodations:

Earth Friendly B&B
17 Olde Noah Hunt Rd.
Cream Ridge, NJ 08514
(609) 259-9744

Southern New Jersey Wine Trail

This region could easily be divided in two, but I've kept it as one for this reason: these wineries all share a growing season moderated by the Atlantic to the east and south, and the Delaware River and Bay to the west and south.

Amalthea, Valenzano, Tomasello, Renault, Sylvin and Balić wineries are each about 20 minutes from each other along U.S. Route 30, so touring the whole bunch in a day or two is relatively easy.

Cape May Winery is the state's southernmost winery, just is over an hour south of Renault, Sylvin and Balić. And Marimac is only an hour southwest of Tomasello or an hour west of Balić. Both are worth the trip, but be sure to call in advance to schedule tastings.

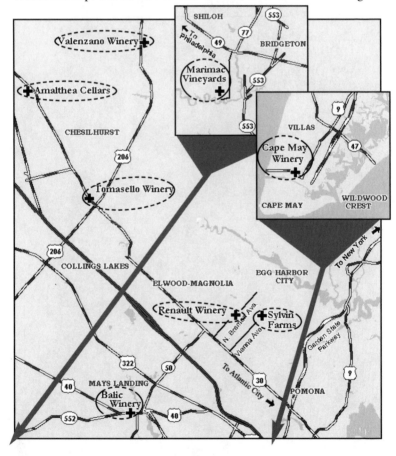

*R*egional Suggestions

Restaurants:

Bait Box Restaurant
30 Handcock Rd.
Greenwich, NJ 08302
(856) 455-2610

Fork's Inn Restaurant
4800 Pleasant Mills Rd.
Hammonton, NJ 08037
(609) 567-8889

Godmother's
413 S. Broadway
Cape May, NJ 08204
(609) 884-4543

Illiano's Restaurant
705 12th St.
Hammonton, NJ 08037
(609) 561-3444

Oyster Bay Steak & Seafood
615 Lafayette St.
Cape May, NJ 08204
(609) 884-2111

Peter Shields Inn
1301 Beach Ave.
Cape May, NJ 08210
(609) 884-9090

Ye Olde Centerton Inn
1136 Almond Rd.
Elmer, NJ 08318
(856) 358-3201

Accommodations:

Angel of the Sea B&B
5 Trenton Ave.
Cape May, NJ 08204
(609) 884-3369

Dr. Jonathan Pitney House
57 North Shore Rd.
Absecon, NJ 08201
(609) 569-1799

Peter Shields Inn
1301 Beach Ave.
Cape May, NJ 08210
(609) 884-9090

Ramada Inn
308 White Horse Pike
Hammonton, NJ 08037
(609) 561-5700

Good Information

Quickly, bring me a beaker of wine,
that I may wet my brain and
say something clever.

— Aristophanies

Wine Festivals

Wine festivals provide a great opportunity for wine lovers to try many different wines without driving all over the region. For a fee, you get to try lots of wine while listening to music and eating great food! And, if you're interested in volunteering at one of the wineries' tents, let them know – they always need help!

Many of the wineries hold their own events, celebrating new wine

releases or using just about any excuse to invite people over for a good time. The Garden State Wine Growers Association organizes wine festivals throughout the summer and most wineries participate.

Sometimes the festivals are hosted by wineries, other times they're off-site. Most of them are themed in some way – a good reason to go to *all* of them!

These folks stomp grapes at a Four Sisters Winery festival.

The major wine festivals are typically held on weekends throughout the summer.

The best way to find out about the festivals is by checking with individual wineries. They will either have pamplets for the festivals or can tell you who to get in touch with for more details.

Also, check the wineries' individual websites or the association's site listed below for up-to-date event listings.

Garden State Wine Growers Association
www.newjerseywines.com

Regional Wine Associations

These associations are good resources for anyone interested in wine, grapes, and the industry as a whole.

American Institute of Wine and Food
1-800-274-AIWF, National Office
contact for local chapters

American Wine Society – National
(716) 225-7613 • aws@vicon.net
contact for local chapters

American Wine Society – New Jersey Regional
Frank C. Aquilino, Vice President
(908) 787-7126 • Aqualante@aol.com

Garden State Wine Growers Association
Members include wineries, grape growers, home winemakers, and general wine enthusiasts.
1-800-524-0043 • www.newjerseywines.com

Rutgers Fruit Research & Development Center
Dr. Joe Fiola
283 Route 539
Cream Ridge, NJ 08514
(609) 758-7311 Ext. 17

Cooperative Extension Rutgers University
Dr. Gary Pavlis
6260 Old Harding Highway
Mays Landing, NJ 08330
(609) 625-0056

These guys are an integral part of New Jersey's wine and grape industry. They're the ones to talk to when deciding what to grow and where to grow it.

New Jersey Wine Industry Advisory Council
Mr. Bill Walker • (609) 292-8853 • william.walker@ag.state.nj.us

Wine Publications & Sites

Magazines:
Wine Enthusiast 1-800-356-8466, www.wineenthusiast.com
Wine Spectator 1-800-395-3364, www.winespectator.com

> Both of these magazines offer reviews of wines and informative articles and columns about wine, wine regions around the world, and general wine appreciation.

Books:
The University Wine Course. Marion W. Baldy.
San Francisco: Wine Appreciation Guild, 1997.

> This is a college text, but it provides wonderful information in a very smart format for anyone interested in furthering a knowledge of wines and winemaking.

Wineries of the Eastern States, 3rd edition. Marguerite Thomas.
Lee, MA: Berkshire House Publishers, 1999.

> This book gives an overview of the wine regions on the Eastern Seaboard while highlighting only a few wineries in each state.

How To Be A Wine Expert. James Gabler.
Baltimore, MD: Bacchus Press, 1995.

> Gabler takes great care to decode the mystery behind wine. Once read, you'll be much more knowledgeable about a broad spectrum of wine topics.

Wine for Dummies 2nd edition. Ed McCarthy. Mary Ewing-Mulligan.
Foster City, CA: IDG Books International, 1998.

> You can't go wrong with this book if you want an introduction to wine. It's written very simply and is a great help for beginning wine drinkers.

Online Sites:
Strat's Place, A Celebration of Wine, Gardening and the Arts.
 www.stratsplace.com

> A non-profit site maintained by Art & Betsy Stratemeyer that includes a massive "World of Wine" section.

Where to Buy New Jersey Wines

Of course, it's always best to buy wine directly from the wineries, but since that's not always the most convenient option, where else can you turn?

Here are the best ways to find your favorite New Jersey wines:

1. The easiest way to get your favorite regional wines is to purchase directly from the winery. If you find something you like, buy it by the case at the winery because most will give a 10-20 percent discount on all case purchases.

2. Buy from the wineries at one of the annual festivals. This is a great opportunity to try many wines and buy as much as you like in one trip.

3. Many of the wineries have their own retail locations throughout the

Unionville's John Altmaier pours wine at a summer festival.

state – usually in restaurants. Check with the individual wineries to find out about their branch locations.

4. If you are a New Jersey resident, you are permitted to have wine shipped directly to your home from the wineries. If you live outside the state, be very wary...many states consider shipping wine for personal use a felony *(write to your elected officials!!!)*. These laws are always changing, so check the law before you attempt to ship anything yourself.

Useful Wine Terms

ACIDITY - the essential natural element that gives wine its crispness on the palate. Too much and the wine will seem hard or bitter. Too little and the wine will seem flabby. Good acid levels help a wine age well.

AFTERTASTE - the taste left in the mouth (good or bad) after the wine has been swallowed.

APPELLATION - a grape growing area designated and governed by the federal government.

AROMA - the fragrance of the grape. What the winemaker does and the wine-making techniques used evolve into nuances of smell that are called "bouquet."

BALANCE - the harmony of all a wine's components – sugar, fruit, tannin, wood, and alcohol. Wines where one or more component stands out and dominates the wine are considered out of balance.

BODY - a wine may be deemed full-bodied, medium-bodied or medium-weight, or light-bodied after an assessment of its weight on the palate. Alcohol, glycerin and sugar all play into a wine's texture and weight.

COMPLEX - one of the most subjective descriptive terms used, a complex wine should have lots of different smells and flavors that seem to change with each sip.

DEPTH - wine with depth has a concentration of flavors, a rich intensity, and tends to be mouth-filling.

DRY - the opposite of sweet. A wine is dry when all of the sugar in the grapes has been fermented into alcohol. The acid content may also determine the sense of dryness.

FINISH - the aftertaste, also called length. All wine has a finish, whether it is short or long, pleasant or unpleasant. A long and/or pleasant finish is preferable to a short and/or unpleasant finish.

FIRST-RUN/FREE-RUN JUICE - when grapes are placed in a press, those that are the ripest will burst on their own. This juice is called "free-run" because it has not actually been pressed from the grapes. Since it is the ripest, most intense juice of the crop, it is typically used as a wine of its own, or blended to improve the rest of the juice once pressed.

FOXY - term often used to describe the earthy, musky character of wines made from North American *labrusca* grapes.

FRUITY - conveying an impression of fruit, sometimes grapes, but often other kinds of fruit, including raspberries, peaches, apricots, cherries, black currants, etc. A fruity wine can be completely dry, with no residual sugar.

FULL-BODIED - wines rich in grape extract, alcohol, and glycerine are full-bodied.

HYBRID - a cross between a hardier native American grape (*labrusca*) variety and one of European descent.

JAMMY - a term describing intensely ripe, rich fruit flavors and aromas in a wine.

LABRUSCA (*vitis labrusca*) - the main North American vine species; extremely resistant to extreme weather conditions and to frost. Examples are Concord and Catawba.

LEGS - after swirling a wine in a glass, it creeps back down the sides of the glass and back into the bowl. Generally, the slower the streaks (legs) are to fall back down, the more full-bodied the wine is. Legs are sometimes called tears, too.

SMOKY - another self-explanatory term, describing the flavor of some barrel-aged wines. Can also be a result of certain soil types.

SMOOTH - self-explanatory term, used to describe the texture and finish of a wine.

SOFT - describes a wine lacking the bite of tannins or acids.

SULFITES - when a label reads "Contains Sulfites," it means sulfur dioxide was used in the process of grape growing or winemaking. Persons allergic to sulfites should be cautious when choosing their wines.

SUR LIE - This term, which in French means "on the lees," means that a wine was aged in contact with the dead yeast cells left over from primary fermentation. Normally, the yeast would be filtered out of the wine, but leaving them in gives the wine a broad, yeasty character.

SWEET - one of the four basic tastes perceived by the tongue, as opposed to the hundreds of flavors that we actually experience with our olfactory senses. The presence of sugar (or occasionally of glycerine) is required to taste sweetness.

TANNIN - This is what makes your mouth pucker when drinking a red wine, especially a young one. It comes from the skins, seeds, and stems of the grapes, and is what gives wine its longevity and dryness.

VARIETAL - a wine made from at least 75 percent of one grape variety.

VINIFERA (*Vitis Vinifera*) - 99 percent of all wines are made from this grape species. There are thousands of varieties of this species, most notably Chardonnay, Cabernet Sauvignon, Merlot, Pinot Noir, Riesling, and Zinfandel.

VINTAGE - the year of a harvest and when the wine was made.

Discover our other titles...

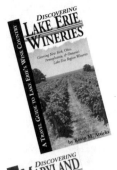

**Discovering
Lake Erie
Wineries**
by Kevin Atticks
ISBN: 0-9668716-3-4
$11.95

**Discovering
Maryland
Wineries**
by Kevin Atticks
ISBN: 0-9668716-0-X
$9.95

***From this hill,
my hand,
Cynthiana's Wine***
by Paul Roberts
ISBN: 0-9668716-2-6
$16.95

Discovering . . . Wineries
by Kevin Atticks
*More titles of this popular series are planned.
Check out website for the latest offerings.*

Thanks for your interest, and we hope you enjoy all of our publications.
For more information, please visit us online at:
www.resonantgroup.com

Send all inquiries to:

resonant publishing

info@resonantgroup.com • www.resonantgroup.com
(603) 462-5675 *fax*